BY NIGEL L. JACKSON

ISB 9798696956558

TABLE OF CONTENTS

INTRO - TRUMPMATIZE DEFINITION   Page 3, 4

BLACK LIVES NEVER MATTERED   Pages 5-7

SUPREMACY CHEMISTRY   Pages 8-11

POLICE, PROSECUTORS, & JUDGES   Pages 12-20

THE EPSTEIN TRAFFIC KING   Pages 21-23

NIGGAS IN NASCARS -   *Pages 24-26*
We Brought Sports Thus Far

AMERICA'S BOSS OF ALL BOSSES   Pages 27-32

FRIENDLY EXTORTIONIST   Pages 33- 37

SALUTING THE SOULS OF SATAN   Page 38-47

THE SCANDALOUS EVANGELISTS   Page 48-49

THE RALLY   Pages 50 – 63

INTRO

The 45th President of The United States, Donald J. Trump, is a genius and truly an American Gangster. I say that with the deepest convictions from my heart. America and the world abroad wasn't ready for the New York native and businessman with Russian ties. His ulterior motives are to divide this great nation and uplift white supremacy and white nationalism. While encouraging Russian interest instead of the county that chose him, which truly under-mines American values.

You're probably wondering why would this writer call Trump of all people a genius? It is my belief that anyone who can trick an entire nation into believing he could lawfully and properly lead them has got to be a brilliant conman. Especially seeing that this man has no political or military experience whatsoever. But he was smart enough as a businessman to sell you him. He marketed, advertised then surrounded himself with people that would be subservient to his views and agendas or else he applies his favorite line from his reality show, "The Apprentice", "You're Fired!"

At the blink of an eye your career and life are downsized you feel cheap, misused, disenfranchised. Violated, a rape victim no mercy, just lies. It's then you realize you've been Trumpmatized.

Vote Biden-Harris 2020. Trumps' plan is to, "Make America Hate Again!"

Trumpmatized:

I.   To be awed and fully committed to the hate, racism, and white supremacy ideologies of Donald J. Trump.

II.   To take part in a nationalistic way of thought. The rule of one group or government in support of White Nationalism and the agenda of Donald J. Trump to "Make America Hate Again!"

"You take the strongest and courageous Black male, the leader of the group. You strip him down naked to humiliate him in front of his people. You beat him down to within an inch of his life. You make sure all the women and children have the best view of what's taking place. You tie one of his arms to a horse. You tie the other arm to a different horse going the opposite direction. You do the same for each leg. You then proceed to whip each of the horses so that they will take off in opposite directions, as an attempt to pull this Blackman's body apart. You then set his body on fire for all of his people to witness." This is the same Willie Lynch mentality that associates with police brutality. They whitemen have been killing black men and women since "the beginning of time." At least since the days of slavery. We were once Kings and Queens until the white man started visiting African tribes showing off his superior firepower that had never been witnessed before in that region. He would get into the chief's head, by telling him that if he acquired this advanced weaponry; his rule, kingdom, and his people's allegiance to him would be secured during his reign.

The whiteman would tell all the chiefs in the region the same story. The only thing that he would want from the chiefs for his weapons of mass destruction was the captives that the chiefs had acquired during war time and they would give the different chiefs the same types of guns. War was inevitable! Every Chiefs ego was exposed whereas, the mentality became keep up or get eaten up. Doing business with the whiteman became a matter of survival and necessity.

Now small issues or differences that would normally get settled in a rational manner would get blown-out of context by the whiteman. He would cause friction between the tribes, minor differences, and tensions, were now considered acts of war. Just for good measure, the Europeans introduced Rum to seal the deal of doom to millions of Africans. We (Africans) at that time had not a clue of the potency, of the consumption and consequences of the liquor, which was a liquid crack to Africans during this time. Just as they have in black communities across America and around the world today. The Europeans strategically introduced guns and drugs as an effort to dismantle the culture and relationships among the tribes of the region.

The chiefs of the region would do whatever they could to satisfy their addictions for guns and drugs. They began to invade neighboring villages to get more captives to get more drugs and guns, from the Europeans.

When the chiefs could not obtain enough captives, they turned on their own people and condemned them to eternal servitude to the whiteman in exchange for more guns and drugs. This is where the ignorant adage, "Black people sold each other into slavery too!" Comes from.

Eventually the chief's kingdoms became weak, their army decimated by being overextended in its efforts to acquire captives from other villages, in this perpetual time of war; that was instigated and manufactured by the whiteman.

The downtrodden chiefs would exchange the strongest of their own people because they fetched the most guns and Rum. The Europeans would then step on the scene to finalize all deals. They would capture all that was left over and enslave the Kings, whom they had originally made the deal with in the first place. This was and still is a timeless, flawless tactic that has been proven, tried and true, since the whiteman first encountered the indigenous people of the world to the present day. Black people do not realize the effect that four hundred years of conditioning, through slavery, has on how they perceive themselves, their lifestyles, the way in which they interact with each other and the systemic impact from white people in general. The whiteman has made himself the ruler, god, and king of all darker people of the world. He has done so through conniving, force, strategy, brainwashing and manipulation.

Hate U is not a state college or university but a state of being, a faculty of one's thoughts. It's a learned behavior. Not something that a person just wakes up one morning and says. "I'm going to commit a hateful act to a person or people that I strongly hate."

It's woven into a person's mind. Normally early in their lives they experience some type of "Trumpmatizing", brainwashing. Which always has a violent curriculum attached to the syllabus. A stone etched set of principles that they abide by a mixture of wicked thoughts or a foundation that they stand on. Here are some of the chemistries that correlate with white supremacy beliefs:

- People who label themselves white make up less than 10% of the world's total population, but control 90% of the world's resources.

- Caucasians have a zero percent birth rate. For every Caucasian that dies, only one Caucasian is born. For everyone person of color that dies, 2 to 3 persons of color are born. Caucasians define their supremacy by the characteristics of their recessive genes, which are the direct result of their lack of melanin.

- In order for the Caucasian race to survive, they must protect their gene pool while destroying the gene pools of all people of color.

- The Black Man's DNA has the potential to annihilate the Caucasian as a race through sexual integration. They believe that they are constantly being attacked by the sun and from the DNA of people of color.

- The Caucasian vows to not go down without a fight.

- The whiteman is driven by his ego or lower self.

- He always knows what's best for everyone at the expense of everyone but himself.

- He will never admit that he is wrong. He will never fully give credit to or listen to a person of color.

- He will never apologize for his mess-ups or actions.

- He will justify what he does or blame the victim.

- The whiteman never forgives but always wants forgiveness from the very people of color he oppresses.

- For him to feel good about himself, he must subject other under his perceived "superior" power.

- Being that Donald J. Trump is a demagogue; a person who appeals to the emotions and prejudices of people specially to gain political power. You will see, if you haven't already, that Trump has a lot in common with those supremacy like ways and ideologies.

They are his base that are carrying out his quest of voter suppression and a "Trump World Order." Which is to bring the world under one rule government and to rewind the clock on systemic racism. A system that was put in place before Trump's new era. Many of Trumps' "supremacist" cult members grew up under hate filled teachings where they grasped the history and origination from which it derived, they become proud. Proud to be a part of a culture that has murdered, robbed, raped, and oppressed people of color for so many centuries. We the poor people of color innocently rush to have our children around them for acceptance. When some white kids have been home schooled to hate you and your children.

I can recall when busing students began in the 80's. I went to high school in my hometown of Columbus, Ohio. My freshman year I attended Beachcroft High.

All the kids from my neighborhood were black we rode the same bus. When we arrived at this state of the art off white structure with tinted windows we were in awe. The houses that surrounded the school were two hundred grand and up. Lawns were neat and crisply manicured. Nothing like we were used to seeing in our community of Brittany Hills. Everyone on the bus was all smiles and wows.

On the school field house roof were words rolled on with what must have been an eighteen-inch paint roller. In big eggshell letters were the words, "Niggers Go Home." We were paralyzed. Our bus driver who was a pretty black woman in her mid-30's at the time stood and faced us with tears in her eyes. I noticed this when she shakily held the buses P.A. system and spoke.

"This is a new way of life for them as it is for you all too. Don't let that..." She pointed to the field house. "Make you a hateful person and stoop to their level. Show them you are better than them."

I was ready to go inside the school and fight some white boys. I grew up boxing in Ohio's Youth Commission I was good with my hands at that age. I was also somewhat aware of the racism at that age too. My grandmother would give me what I look back and refer to now as, "Racial Education." She would make jokes to me like, "I'm going to be on T.V. at four o'clock." Then she'd sit on top of the floor model T.V. at exactly four. I recall one time she said to me, "Nigel you better beware of white folks. They will lie to you, steal form you and will kill you if they catch you out of place in their neck of the woods".

I just sat there listening attentively shook my head and said, "Yes Big Mama."

So when I saw the writing on the field house at Beachcroft that to me was what Big Mama had warned me about. It also makes me wonder. If my grandmother would make it a point to racially educate me what did the parents of the children who wrote "Niggers Go Home" who hate for no reason tell them?

I say no reason because my grandmother who was in her late 70's when she passed, her parents, parents more than likely were slaves. And Big Mama most definitely was a part of the racially motivated civil rights movements. So how could Big Mama not give me knowledge of her firsthand experiences of dealing with these people?

What's so baffling to me is how can white people who have done so much wrong to black people still hate us? Please vote we can't let Trump win our lives depend on it, he wants to "Make America Hate Again."

I was nearly murdered by police when I was seven years old. We were living in Lincoln Park apartments. A project on Columbus, Ohio's southside. Like most inner-city Urban housing communities Lincoln Park or "The Jets" a name we later tagged it, was encased by industrious loud smoat spewing factories. Owens Corning a fiber glass making plant, federal glass as well as Buckeye Steel. Just beyond Buckeye Steel sits the entire city's trash and human waste site. So, you always heard drills, jacks, and train tracks at all hours of the night and day, with a constant smell of shit as a chaser.

This was it for my mother, four sisters and me the baby boy. My mother had already been deeply immersed in a happy relationship with my stepfather who I now call my dad since I was two years of age. He had two of his three children living with him at this particular time, Alice and Timmy. Tim who was one year and three days older than me was my pal.

Tim and I would walk along the train tracks that ran behind the Jets. Owen Corning was expanding their factory. The area was littered with potato chip bags, lunch debris and glass pop bottles. The bottles were returnable. Meaning we could return the bottles back to the grocery store and get fifteen to twenty cents per bottle. There were maybe sixteen to twenty bottles, we could've made a few dollars. Which would have been a decent amount of money for seven and eight year old's in the 70's.

Damn that! Tim and I started bursting the bottles. Tim showed me his skyhook against a wall that was eight feet away. I showed him my no look then he threw two from a football center snapping stance. This went on for a few minutes until it was nothing left but shard glass. I heard a car door open and peeked around the corner of the new construction.

"It's the fuzz!" I said, Tim without hesitation took off running back down the railroad tracks. Tim had always been a fast kid. That speed would later place him in the NFL. Which I talk about in my book, "Can U C It Now?" Tim was at least twenty yards ahead of me on the tracks looked back and yelled "Come on Nigel he's going to kill us!"

I sped up as fast as I could. My asthma was stronger than my fear. I couldn't make it and I knew it. There were too many tracks ahead in an open clearance. I looked back at the cop he was on one knee aiming his gun directly at me. The explosive thunderous sounds were deafening to my little ears. The beats I heard were fast repetitions of my heart. I turned around the blood rushing through my veins was cold. I started running fast as my youthful legs would allow. But I was running towards the officer pleading,

"Please don't shoot us please!"

The officer was still in his shooters position on one knee, with one eye closed, ready to kill me. I kept approaching and he lowered his weapon, and I opened my arms and hugged him tightly. That was in the 70's. Unfortunately, too many black men and women have been murdered by the police since then. Whether we are jogging like Ahmad Arbery, sleeping like Breonna Taylor or going to the corner store like George Floyd, we are hunted.

This is one of the reasons that black youth don't dislike the police, they hate the police because of all the havoc they've reaped upon the black communities. Members of the black communities say we need to "defund the police" to end as chaos and anarchy. The outlet paints a narrative of criminals running wild, rampant violent crimes and mayhem in the streets. The Republicans say defunding police will cause more harm to black and brown communities and that the calls are dangerous, reckless, and wrong. How can this be true when the police are the problem? I'm not suggesting to totally take the police out of the black and brown communities. I believe having more blacks in police departments around America is a logical solution. Because at some point we must be the police that we want to police us. We can't keep asking police thatdon't understand us or care for us to police us. We have plenty of young black people that are more than qualified to become police officers. There would be less shootings and more realistic arrest. Often white officers trump up the charges to get a defendant to cop-out to lesser charges when all they really had was lesser charges from the beginning.

Even if we defund or reallocate money to develop our own communities with the officers that we want to see, we must stop asking other people to change. They haven't changed in all of these years; they will continue to murder us and instill fear to keep us from voting and standing up against them. They don't care or realize that they are "Trumpmatized."

-Verifiable Facts-

- Black people make up 13.2 percent of the United States population but represent 24.2 percent of the deaths from police use of firearms.

- Since 2005, No judge has ever convicted an officer of murder or man slaughter while using lethal force in the line of duty.

- Ninety-nine percent of killings by police from 2013 to 2019 have not resulted in officers being charged with a crime.

There is an unholy alliance between prosecutors and police. Altering a prosecutor's relationship with police isn't a simple or easy reform, for instance it would be a fundamental shift in the way our criminal justice system would work. In fact, the justice system is designed to insulate police officers when their actions result in death. The legal system tends to give a presumption of good faith to officers. Regardless of whose life the officer may have taken.

When you connect U.S. actions even beyond its borders, one must come to the conclusion that the U.S. in fact is the number one international violator of human rights. This racist element of law enforcement has been here from the beginning and people have lost their lives from the beginning of this country. However, the number overall of hate crimes has remained steady following a three-year increase after the election of Donald Trump: Which is a backlash to the presidency of Barack Obama, helping fuel the current climate of racial hatred. Trumps racially charged rhetoric has given a green light to white supremacists and crooked cops whose threats and actions primarily targeted black people.

According to 2018 FBI statistics, 53.6 percent of the offenders who committed 6,266 hate crimes against other people were white and predominately male. The FBI analysis said among single bias hate crime incidents in 2018 motivated by race and ethnicity, 47.1 percent were anti-black bias.

During the protest after the killing of George Floyd there were many white supremacist breaking windows and vandalizing properties near peaceful protestors areas. The reason they were doing this was to give Trump an excuse to say the protestors were causing problems. And that there needs to be more law and order. It's no coincidence that wherever there was peaceful protest the police would be there also, after being dog whistled from Trump to pepper spray and fire rubber bullets at the protestors.

Then the anti-protestors, military police, National Guards, FBI, and U.S. Marshalls would be present too! They were kidnapping protestors, snatching them off the streets without merit or cause. Well the cause is voter suppression to make people not want to vote. If you don't get out and vote against this monster and his "Trumpmatized" followers, we will be under a "Trump World Order." This is where one government will rule the world. You won't have any freedom or liberty whatsoever. As of right now war has been waged against people of color. This has been in existence unbeknownst to many people of color for the last 50 - 60 years.

After Dr. King was assassinated you seen a drastic shift in whites' attitudes about race. The effects did not persist and lead to real change. The civil unrest, images of looters burning cities and angry black people allowed a huge white backlash to occur.

The backlash led to significantly more whites dismissing the efforts of civil rights leaders and groups. It did the opposite of what it was supposed to do. Whites engaged in behaviors that they had commonly shown when blacks made even a modicum of progress in America; they showed how unhappy they were and fought against it.

Trump is just one of America's last, "Great White Hopes" to maintain the American Dream of an all-white everything, schools, neighborhoods and workplaces. Anybody with a little commonsense would know this frame of thought is virtually impossible. Because blackmen particularly are going to be anywhere a white woman might be. "Trumpminites" are thinking about a civil war. Why do you think these people have been stock piling guns and bullets? The crooked cops are just the frontline of their "American Greatness" or "American Hatefulness." If you were to ask one of their members, "Why do you hate black people?" They couldn't give you a legitimate reason other than that's what they were taught. Which is why Trump brought with him record numbers of death threats, actual death plots and a deep sense of white distress and victimhood. Mr. Trump fed and rode those feelings to the White House and unapologetically feeds the lumbering beast regularly.

When I listened to the 2019 democratic presidential hopefuls and their policies and promises they would've implemented had they been selected to "De-Trumpmatize" America the two things that I looked at were: What they were saying and what they've done. Kamala Harris who is now on the ticket with Joe Biden who is running against Donald Trump for the United States presidential seat. Mrs. Harris said she is willing to talk about prison reform and help fix the injustices and disparities done by the DOJ.

How can she not want to fix a system she once endorsed as an ex-prosecutor and Attorney General of the State of California?

Prosecutors are persecutors too! They will cause or inflict harm because of your beliefs and will indict without evidence. They are the justice system authorities responsible for ensuring that all receive justice irrespective of color, class, or creed. Prosecutors historically refused to hold police accountable for illegal brutality which contributes to the continuation of abuses.

Despite the fact that the Minnesota police force has a lengthy history of excessive force and police brutality dating back to the 90's. The prosecuting attorney elected in 1998 refused to file charges in over two dozen fatal police brutality related incidents during that prosecuting attorney's tenure. That prosecutor also refused to file charges against the policeman who killed George Floyd when that policeman was involved in a non-fatal incident of brutality. That prosecuting attorney was Amy Klobuchar, a U.S. Senator from Minnesota who is an unsuccessful candidate for the Democratic Party 2020 presidential candidacy. Had she done the right thing and prosecuted Derek Chauvin, George Floyd would still be alive.

But prosecutors are not held accountable and nobody judges the judges! The crooked cops hand over the crooked case to that crooked prosecutor and goes on the bench of the crooked judge. The Supreme Court is supposed to be the gate keepers of justice in America. However, it has effectively closed its doors to claims of bias at every stage of the criminal justice process, from stop and search to plea bargaining and sentencing. Which gives support and much validity to "The Dred Scott Doctrine" that states, "The Black Man has no rights which the white man is bound to respect."

Thanks to the supreme court of the United States it gives the "Dred Scott Doctrine" a stay of execution. Do to this fact the infamous doctrine still silently lurks in the shadows of racial injustice in America today.

I'm sorry Kamala, unless the person is cooperating with a prosecutor, I've never heard of anyone having a good outcome, when dealing with a prosecutor. I do understand that the laws are the laws and must be abided by. But from a convicted/victim standpoint this system thrives off massively incarcerating the poor, black, brown and sometimes innocent I have a problem with that. I know I've made my own choices and decisions to get here to this federal prison I'm writing this book from.

However, I have been wrongly charged in a State of Ohio death penalty case. It was two overzealous prosecutors that pursed the case. I wrote a book about it titled, "Can U C It Now?" which is aimed at bringing my friends' true killer to justice. I say this to say that. The policies and procedures are put in place to protect prosecutors. Say if a prosecutor wrongfully charges a man and he gets sentenced to death. Then after so many years and failed appeals he gets put to rest.

Later the man's family attorney finds that the police lied, and the witnesses were coerced by the prosecutors who purposely withheld evidence. Evidence that could've proven the man's innocence. Do you think the prosecutor is going to admit that they were wrong? Me either!

Nothing happens to the prosecutor. They aren't responsible for the man's wrongful conviction or death. So what the family might get awarded a little bit of money. Their loved one has still been murdered.

I don't want you to think I have something against Senator Harris. I believe in my heart that she may very well be a good person. I really do. But I don't believe that a person can be one way for so many years and change overnight. If this isn't true. Why is it when a defendant goes to sentencing and says, "Your Honor, I know my attorney and prosecutor have reached a deal of ten years for me having a few bullets in my glove compartment. And I'm a felon. Who's not allowed to be around ammunition. Since I have been awaiting my sentencing, I found God and I have changed. I can't do all of that time."

The judge tells the man. "I understand that you are 65 years old and ten years is a life sentence at your age. But! Like you said. You found God and I'm sure he'll be wherever you do your time. So, you do what you can and He'll do the rest."

As well as "Qualified Immunity." Like the "Dred Scott Doctrine" has no legitimate foundation. The rule provides that the victims whose constitutional rights were violated can't sue police officers or other government officials for damages unless the actions were so egregious that no reasonable officer would believe them lawful. In practice, it means that countless violations go entirely unremedied. The history of "Qualified Immunity" offers no principled answer. The Supreme Court created the doctrine in the 1967 case Pierson v. Ray, in which a group of clergymen were arrested for attempting to integrate a segregated coffee shop at a Mississippi bus terminal. They sued the arresting officers under a provision of the 1871 Ku Klux Klan Act that authorized lawsuits seeking compensation for constitutional violations. The court held that the officers who arrested the clergymen should escape liability if they acted in good faith, thus introducing the rule that would become known as "Qualified Immunity."

Police officers, prosecutors, government officials and judges are bound by the Constitution; they should not be shielded from accountability when they violate one's constitutional rights.

This is why Donald J. Trump wants to put his "Trumpmatized" people in places of power so that they can continue to adjudicate. If they can adjudicate, they can discriminate, if they can discriminate my friend, they can "Make America Hate Again!"

THE EPSTEIN
TRAFFIC KING

The truth about Trump and Jeffery Epstein's ties died inside a New York Federal Detention Center.

Jeffery Epstein was an American self-made multi-millionaire. Who was arrested for alleged sex trafficking of underaged girls. These charges stemmed from Epstein's plea agreement with prosecutors in the early 2000's, in Palm Beach, Florida. A deal that his dozens of accusers had no knowledge of. Which they one were too young to follow up on, and the deal was reached in private before he plead guilty in the state's court.

Afterwards he was required to register as a sex offender and pay restitution to some of his victims. While he was sentenced to serve a 13-month jail term, Epstein was permitted to leave the jail to work for twelve hours a day, six days a week.

There is too much footage of Trump attending parties that were hosted by the alleged convicted sex trafficker of underaged girls for Trump not to have know this was going on.

Do you think for one second that many of the "privileged politicians" have not engaged in sex parties with drugs and prostitutes? Or did you think that Marion Barry and Bill Clinton were the only two?

As for Trump he's been married three times. We know he will lie to, steal from and cheat on anybody. Although I've never been married, I have had large sums of money. I know that is does afford you power and an invincible mentality, and it's most definitely an allure for women. Which makes it hard for a man to keep his penis in his pants.

So, imagine Donald and Jeffery together with what has been said as "a room full of beautiful women." Drugs, alcohol, and Viagra everybody's "naked and not afraid," they're on Jefferies Island with white sand, palm trees and bamboo fire sticks. A full moon is illuminating the crest of the earth that's surrounded by ocean as far as the human eye can see. They have four girls a piece biting, rubbing, sucking and pulling on their old stinking white asses. Is Don going to stop them and look over at Jeffery to ask, "How old are they?"

These types of sick sex scandals have been going on for years involving. Trump's, Epstein's, Weinstein's, and all types of nasty beings like R. Kelly. The statement, "He likes his on the younger side." Validates that Trump knew about Jefferies sick fetish, for little girls traumatization the madness must end don't let him

"Make America Hate Again."

SALUTING THE SOULS
OF SATAN

He salutes the soldiers of Satan. "I thank God every day that Donald J. Trump is president and will launch a race war and crusade." - Trumpmatized Person

Being a hate filled person not only takes one in this instance to be Trumpmatized it also takes one who has surrendered their soul to the devil. Take a look at the average age of these massive shooters they range from 21-30ish. At those ages, their minds haven't even fully developed. They are still impressionable and able to be molded into an evil demonic saturated being. They read books like "The Turner Diaries" by William Pierce that spoke highly about white supremacy and murdering Blacks, Jews & government bombings.

That book is the white supremacist bible. And in many of their homes and sanctuaries you will find a copy of the book. Along with a picture of Timothy McVeigh the 1995 OKC bomber. He was responsible for 160 death's 19 were children. These young whites praise him and those like Hitler who were mass murders. People actually worship these men as the Evangelicals believe Trump is being used as a vessel to do the will of God. It makes you wonder what God would promote a people to murder innocent women and children that they don't even know. By Donald Trump rationalizing the acts of hate done at the hands of "Satan's Soldiers" by not condemning them and their white supremacist beliefs he's emitting them to carry them out. Now you are seeing more and more young white men who are infatuated with massive shootings. Some are getting arrested before they get the chance to carry the act out. Some are not.

"It's not the gun that pulls the trigger, it's the person." Trump wants you to believe… It's not the gun it's the people that get a hold of the guns. These people have serious mental illnesses. We need to re-open mental health centers like we used to have."

What he is doing if you pay attention is swinging his hypnosis pendulum tongue to your ears. Which will translate to your mind so that you will overlook the big picture and become Trumpmatized.

Once you are Trumpmatized you lose focus as if you are so in love with that loser boyfriend and you know he isn't going to get a job or stop cheating. But you don't want to leave cause the sex is so good. You begin to think that you can't do any better because this creep has verbally and financially abused you beyond repair. Your self-esteem immerses into a childlike state to where you are dependent upon him and your future retirement and 401k plans look dim. Yet, he tells you, "You'd better stick with me or your 401k is going to be dead." Sound familiar? That is the effect that he has on people. What I get out of that statement is the NRA has him by the balls and they helped put him in office. Plus, he can't take the guns away from his cult members who have vowed to carry out the master plan, which is to launch a race war and crusade. A crusade by definition means. Any of the military expeditions undertaken by Christian powers in the 11th, 12th, and 13th centuries to win the Holy Land from the Muslims. Another thing I get from that statement. When he says, "These people have some serious mental issues. We need to   re-open mental health centers like we used to have."

Years ago, a person close to you cold admit you into a mental health center and leave you there until they felt that you were stable. So, he's setting it up so that a person like the El Paso shooter could be admitted and in 2 or 3 years be declared mentally stable and get released. Or Trump could give him a pardon for these same reasons. He's already giving him a defense. Others will get the same. In my opinion anyone who drives 10 hours to a community where you know the people that you hate are is totally sane. So, imagine what the other white domestic terrorists are going to do when they find out they will be admitted to mental health centers. Also if Congress implements extensive background checks as they have been talking about for the last 20 years. This will mean the independent gun-trade and show dealers will get stuck with the guns they buy in bulk from the NRA. Which in turn would slow down profits for gun manufacturers. That will affect the income and outcome of the legislator's pockets. Which are lined by layers of loot the gun lobbyist puts in them. Would you pay someone to shovel your snow if you lived in Miami? Or would you pay someone to campaign against you if it were to cost you billions of dollars a year?

The point is they aren't going to stop paying politicians and the politicians aren't going to stop accepting the payments. No matter how many mass shootings we have in America.

This is why they want to "Make America Hate Again."

NIGGIAS IN NASCARS

We Brought Sports Thus Far

When we were product of the Atlantic Slave Trade.
We were niggas to waste.

When we took our speed to Olympic tracks
we became niggas to race.

In the remake of the move "Star Wars"
we were called Niggas in space.

Now that "Bubba Wallace" is in Nascar
we'll be the niggas to chase!

STILL A NIGGA!

"Wouldn't you like to see one of their NFL team owners. Tell one of them players that don't stand for the National Anthem disrespecting our American flag, "You're fired you son of a bitch. You're fired!"

That's what Donald J. Trump had to say about athletes like Colin Kaepernick who took a knee in 2016. That brother was not trying to disrespect the flag; he was disturbed over the police killings of Black and Brown American Citizens outside of the law justice and he wanted to draw attention to it. Because all of the evil we have suffered, we suffered it under the confederate flag, but we suffered it mostly under the American flag.

September 1. 2016 Colin Kaepernick took a knee when the flag was presented, and the National Anthem was played. It's not that Black people hate the flag, as such; they don't hate America as such, but just as Kaepernick wanted, there was and still is a need of attention drawn to the suffering we've endured under both flags.

The recent 2020 murders Ms. Breonna Taylor, Mr. George Floyd and Rayshard Brooks who all were unarmed. Attributes to Kaepernick's reason to kneel because every cop that shot those innocent Black people have an American flag somewhere on their uniforms.

As for the confederate flag, rightfully so governors around the United States demanded that they be taken down because it's insulting to Black people. Because we were slaves picking cotton for white people under that flag. Now Blacks want them to take the flag down. Do you know how having to take the flags down are hurting, "Trumpmatized" white people? The confederate flag would fly over every Nascar track before a race. It has been stopped because of the recent demands by Black people and governors. Which angered many because that's part of their evil history that they didn't want to let go of.

Many white people from the south fought to keep Black people enslaved under that flag. And many Black lives were lost in the Civil war under that flag.

As for the American flag before every sporting event in the United States or if an American athlete is playing anywhere on the planet that flag is flown, and the National Anthem is sung. The first line of "The National Anthem" states: "Oh say, can you see, by the dawns early light..." Francis Scott Key was a racist: he was a hater of Black people. You only hear the edited version of "The National Anthem". The third stance is the one where he wrote racist melodies. Because many Blacks fought on the side of the south, others fled North and fought on the side of the North. As well as in the war for American independence 6,000 Blacks fought on the side of the British. And the British gave them refuge in Canada. So, when Francis Scott Key saw the flag waving, he

started talking about those Blacks that were fighting on the side of Britain against both of those flags.

The confederate flag became a recognized prop for the Ku Klux Klan which was founded in 1865 in Pulaski, Tennessee, by six confederate veterans.

At first the original Klansmen simply dressed as ghosts and goblins to play pranks on neighbors, but the joke turned serious and ugly as others joined the organization and used it to terrorize former slaves and political opponents to implement voter suppression.

The key to its success was the broadening of its original white supremist stance to include other popular American prejudices at the time. Catholics, Jews, immigrants, labor unionists and liberals joined African Americans on the Klan's hate list. At a time when many white Americans fretted about internal enemies undermining the American way of life. Klansmen presented themselves as defenders of "100 percent Americanism" against all comers. Publicly Klansmen pursed their agenda through boycotts and voting drives; violence and intimidation aimed against Klan's enemies formed the more covert dimension of Klan activity, publicly denied by the national leadership just as it is today by President Trump but tacitly approved by them and carried out by local Klansmen under the white Klan mask.

It took the Civil Rights struggle of the 1950's and 1960's to breathe new life in the Klan. Challenged by school desegregation and swelling demands of Black Americans for equal rights, while white southerners clinging to the Jim

Crow system of racial privilege turned to the Klan. In an attempt to turn back the clock. just as Trump is attempting to do in the next 4 years if re-elected. This is how many of the NBA and NFL owners feel they look at these black men as meat. Just as they used to have the black slaves stand on stages looking for the ones with the most brute strength and muscle mass as well as reproductivity. Today it's called "The NFL Combines." This is where they check for the fastest running, highest jumping, most agile negroes on the planet. After these highly physical rigorous test are done the negro is auctioned off to the highest bidding Slave Master through his agent/slave broker under contract.

Sports needs us we don't need sports, but we are so damn good at them as black athletes. Where do you think basketball would be today without Wilt Chamberlin, Dr. J, Kareem, Magic, or Michael Jordan? The Negro Basketball Association is what it should be called. Look at the economic empowerment that comes from basketball alone. The jersey sells, shorts, caps, and equipment that schools, little leagues, and colleges are consumers of yearly. Nike wouldn't be in business if it weren't for Michael Jordan. I feel that of the 32 teams in basketball and football there should be 16 Black owned teams in both sports. Seeing that 75% of the players of those sports are Black Men.

Bubba Wallace is Nascar's newest negro and first Black driver. As a welcoming to Nascars 2020 race season a lynching noose was placed in the garage where his car was kept. Trump said he believes it was a hoax. Just like that! Without any investigation or support. Because Bubba Wallace is a Black Man and Trump's thoughts are that of a racist slave master. Whenever there are incidents with Black people period, he's going to show his racist ass.In the early 2000's the popularity of Nascar started to diminish somewhat. Pop Culture was being overshadowed by the Hip

Hop Culture. Dale Earnhardt Jr. was in videos with rapper T.I. and Jay Z along with Dana Fitzpatrick.

Now we are starting to see the determination displayed by white millennials in the vanguard of the recent protest. Which attest to the fact these young white millennials aren't beholden to the hatred inhibitions of their forbearers. The cultural bonds between black and white Americans have been so thoroughly cemented by way of sports and Hip Hop. White millennials see no distinction between black suffering and white suffering. To them the George Floyd murder was not viewed as simply a black tragedy but an American tragedy.

As for Donald Trump and his "Trumpmatized" syndicate patient morale of faith has run its course. Symbolic victories and tokenism have lost their prideful luster. A racially fatigued "Crippled America" by the Trump Administration can no longer be tolerated.

Jay Z, Bubba Wallace, Lebron James possess the cultural power that has arisen out of centuries of brutality, betrayal, and broken promises, to become the most powerful force in the world! Trump and his followers have failed to realize that the reason the world loves America is because or Black people's swag and our cultural influences. Trump and his supporters aren't cool. You don't see other countries trying to duplicate redneck hillbilly shit! Blues, Hip Hop, Jazz, Rock and Roll are all art forms created by African Americans.

The world is enamored with American culture because of African Americans. That's one of the reasons there were protest around the world. Because the rest of the world and America know all that we have done for this country and we are the Magic Makers of it.

Young millennials of all races and backgrounds unlike past generations will not be fooled by America's unmerited mirage of false racial hope. They have taken to the streets demanding meaningful, long-lasting change, right now! And many older white folks are tired of hating people of color for nothing. They grew up loving our music, witnessed black athlete's break records in every sport we've played. Now we have a Nigga In Nascar!

Bubba Wallace is backed by Dr. Dre's, "Beats by Dre" speaker company. So, you know when Bubba takes a victory lap blurring, "Fuck Da Police" out of his speakers, it's like running a marathon in mud against Trumps racial tactics of hate.

This race we can't let him win, to "Make America Hate Again."

AMERICA'S BOSS OF ALL BOSSES!

Gangsters make the world go 'round. Charles "Lucky" Luciano was aware of this fact, as he gunned down leading rivals to forcefully inherit The American Mafia Crime Syndicate which was set in place by Al Capone. While Capone was away in prison serving a two-year stint for tax evasion, this brought blood money and opportunity to "Lucky" Luciano and his right-hand man Meyer Lansky. Together they went on to become the architects of modern organized crime. Since the 1860's, the Mafia quickly learned to control local voters, and struck alliances with political parties delivering votes on demand. Despite occasional bursts of persecution, the tacit bargain between the Mafia and the government has remained a fixture of Italian politics since that time.

The key to the system pioneered by Luciano and Lansky was a remixing of Mafia activities away from the small time rackets of its early days into the immense profits to be gained from legitimate businesses, gambling casinos, international drug trading, and prostitution. Lansky played a central role in the blackmail scheme that turned F.B.I. head J. Edgar Hoover, a homosexual with a taste for cross-dressing, into an ally of organized crime. Lansky succeeded in obtaining photos of Hoover and used them to force the F.B.I. Chief to take the heat off and as Trump would say "downplay" organized crime. So much so that Hoover's repeated public insistence convinced America that there was no organized crime problem, and his refusal to use F.B.I. assets against the Mafia was the quid-pro-quo that kept Lansky and his associates from releasing the photos to the press and destroying Hoover's career.

Donald J. Trump out maneuvering other very rich and powerful competitors in their thirsty bids to own lucrative

Atlantic City casinos illustrates how gangsters do make the world go 'round! Close ties to East Coast mobsters are what set Trump apart from Mafioso's who were hell bent on owning A.C. casinos. Nothing moved in Atlantic City in the late seventies and eighties without the permission of Little Nicky Scarfo, the murderous Godfather of the Philadelphia - Atlantic City Mafia at the time.

In the late sixties, Philly mob boss Angelo "The Gentle" Don Bruno had had enough of Scarfo's murderous antics and exiled the young hot head to Atlantic City. So, when gambling was legalized in Atlantic City, Scarfo, who'd already ruled with an iron fist, instantly became a major player because he controlled the over and underworld.

New York's five families, having everything to gain, arranged for the murder of "The Gentle" who held a seat on The Commission, and was simply too powerful to muscle out. With Bruno out of the way, The Commission promoted Scarfo as head of the Philadelphia - Atlantic City Mafia. Knowing his upgrade to Godfather would make Scarfo forever indebted to New York's five families.

The next move by the Mafia was to implant one of their own; someone they could trust to ensure their cut of the Atlantic City casino rackets; a front man and legitimate businessman, their fellow New Yorker - Donald Trump!

Not long after the Donald Trump - Nicky Scarfo partnership was set in motion, Nicky Scarfo went on murderous rampages, while Mr. Trump was on a different kind of rampage. He displaced scores of poor black families from their homes to build his casinos.

Trump milked his creditors out of tens of millions of dollars, and they feared Scarfo, who was charged with the murder of a judge and acquitted in court. With a man like that backing his play, creditors knew when to cut their losses.

America loves crime stories because America is a crime story. Who knew "The Teflon Don", John Gotti would bring the glitz, glamour, and cameras to organized crime? He made crime cool. Hollywood made millions off Gotti's allure and swag, "Forget about it!" Stars became "Made" through the likes of Gottiism.

"Mobsters", "Good Fella's", "Donnie Brascoe", and "The Sopranos" were Mafia spin off films inspired by some of Gotti's real-life experiences.

The Federal RICO (Racketeering In Criminal Organizations) statute was the demise of organized crime and was used on other crime families by prosecutor Rudy Giuliani. Then on John Gotti, who beat the Federal Government twice at trial with his attorney Bruce Cutler who at the time was a court room mastermind.

Gotti was charged and tried a third time without Cutler. Due to Cutler being heard on F.B.I. wiretaps in conversation with Gotti, the courts deemed Cutler a conflict of interest. At trial, Gotti was found guilty and sentenced to multiple life sentences. He eventually died in federal prison.

Only one person loves the cameras as much as John Gotti did. Trump! He loved the attention and boss status quite well. In fact, "The Apprentice" was a hit for Trump telling people "You're Fired!".

Trump one-upped all his crime predecessors with a term in what turned out to be America's biggest brothel, The

White House. He made Rudy Giuliani his personal attorney. Why not, he co-authored the RICO on bosses. "You can't beat 'em, make 'em join you!" was Trump's thinking. He also has America's Top Cop in his back pocket, The United States Attorney General - William Barr, who has had ample time and opportunity to indict Trump for everything from extortion to murder. Yes murder!

An over-the-phone interview with Journalist Bob Woodward, Trump confessed to the danger that COVID-19 would bring to the world. He discussed in great detail the difference of COVID being more deadly and contagious because it's not just contractible when someone touches you, but it is airborne. He also talks about how people of any age can get it and it's something this world has never seen before. Being that Trump is the leader of the country and has over 65 million Trumpmatized Tweeter followers that will kill anybody, including themselves, if it means saving him; he's responsible for them too.

Since he withheld the aforementioned information, plus he doesn't wear a mask and his followers fight tooth and nail against state and local medical recommendations to wear masks. Then he lied again telling the public the virus couldn't affect young children. Yet people of all ages have died from the disease. When told the virus had already killed over 150,000 people, he stated "It is what it is."

Donald Trump should have been indicted for every death resulting from the COVID-19 virus. If I were to rob a bank with a fellow bank robber and a fierce shootout occurred, us versus the bank's security, and security shoots and kills the guy I'm with, I get charged with his murder because I knowingly took him into life threatening circumstances.

The same applies to Trump because he knew how deadly and life threatening the Corona virus was, yet he took Americans into those circumstances.

What makes Trump any different from Hitler killing Jewish people or Saddam who killed his own people or slave owners who killed millions of black people? Murder is murder!

The government shutdown was the biggest heist in American history. What better way to get money than have congress members sign over a check for 6 billion dollars? For a wall that who is going to measure the distance and materials used to make it? You don't think Trump got a kick-back? This is what makes him the best organized criminal but worst president ever in my opinion:

He took pages from Al Capone's book of tax evasion, Nicky Scarfo's book of murder, Luciano and Lansky's book of blackmail and control of the F.B.I. chief, and John Gotti's take them to trial because they're "Trumpmatized" by your style.

Do you think Trump will go to jail like Al Capone for tax evasion? "Forget about it" or like Gotti for the RICO? "Forget about it." Will he admit there's a domestic terrorist threat from White Supremacists? "Forget about it."

Do you think if Trump wins, he'll "Make America Hate Again"? "Are you kidding me?"

Pinky and The Brain withheld the aid to Ukraine. President Donald J. Trump and his personal attorney Rudy Giuliani conspired to a smear campaign against presidential nominee Joe Biden. The president was on a phone call with the president of Ukraine Volomyer Zenlensky on July 25th, 2019. During that call President Trump asked him to do him a favor. To investigate his number one competitor Joe Biden.

The thing that's really senseless on Trump part is the call as all calls to foreign powers are listened to by officials from both countries. A "whistleblower" someone from within the Trump camp said they heard the call, and it was very disturbing. This among plenty of other underhanded schemes and tricks led to "The Path to Impeachment." Not long after "the call" Nancy "Peloconstictor" Pelosi had already had the impeachment inquiry underway. The "Inquiry" is an investigation to round-up enough facts to impeach: to bring an accusation against. To charge with a crime or misdemeanor of (a public official) before a competent tribunal with misconduct in office.

Trump in the interim was sending his loyal base to find out who was now his disloyal enemy. Through news press conferences and Twitter he called his sixty-five million plus, "Trumpmatized" followers to a call of action or to inflict harm to the whistle-blower. With statements like, "In the good old days when we were smart, we used to deal with people like the whistle-blower much differently." Then Trump placed a $50,000 bounty for the identity of the whistleblower. Trump loyalist Gurrado Rivera stated, "I would like to fight the rotten snitch."

Trump should have known better than asking another foreign power to interfere with the American election process. Especially after being accused of having Russia get involved when he won against Hillary Clinton in 2016. He made a boneheaded move by yelling "Russia if you're listening please find the emails!" He was referring to the over ten thousand emails of Hillary Clinton's that were lost. The emails if found were supposed to be evidence that Hillary was doing illegal business with other countries as well. Which would be of no surprise to any living level minded person that knows some of the Clinton's criminal history.

How certain men and their families became rich overnight are fascinating stories. To show how it works, think of an American family that used to own a few little five and dime stores in Arkansas. That family has five siblings in the top ten charts of wealthiest people in America. The family is the Walton's of Walmart and Sam's Club. A little digging into the way Sam Walton went from small store owner to multi-billionaire is very shocking. The man who financed Walton in his Walmart and Sam Club enterprises was Jackson Stephen's, a multi-billionaire.

The records reveal that Stephens owns many corporations, one of which is a bank in Mena, Arkansas where billions of dollars of drug money were laundered. Stephen and an Indonesian by the name of James Riady used this bank almost exclusively for laundering the Mena, Clinton, George Bush (the father) drug money that came into the Mena Airport. This money was from the guns for drugs sales that more going on between the bureaucrats in Washington and the Sandinistas of Nicaragua - The Enemy Unmasked, second edition, Bill Hughes, Truth Triumphant p. 138-139.

Clinton while governor of Arkansas, which is Rockefeller's backyard, got involved with the elite's drug running. Nella and Mena Airports in southwest Arkansas were part of the drug running system that is related to the Iran, Contra scandal. A reporter from a small newspaper in a small Arkansas town asked why Larry Nichols worked for the Arkansas Development finance Authority. The question seems innocent enough, but the answer began to uncover the whole web of intrigue that involved the drug running and illegal arms shipments to Central America that both Bush and Clinton were involved in. - Fritz Springmeier, Bloodlines of the Illuminati, Ambassador House p. 326.

Stephens had used much of this money to finance both Republican George Bush and Democrat Bill Clinton in their respective presidential campaigns. Not only did Stephens use the drug money for presidential campaigns, but so much money came into Arkansas that the Attorney General and the Governor Bill Clinton along with Stephens and his company, began putting it into businesses that had images of being patriotic Americans. Walmart was one of many businesses that benefited. Two other companies, that came into prominence during the reign of Stephens and Clinton in Arkansas, were Hunt Trucking and Tyson Foods. Tyson Foods, which has become known as the "Chicken King" of America, even stooped so low as to stuff chickens with drugs and then send them across America.

One of the board members of Walmart for years was Hillary Clinton. She also served as Walmart's Chief Counsel.

So what does this have to do with someone being, "Trumpmatized?"

"One Nation Under A Groove," see Bill Clinton is the cousin of George Clinton from the group "The Parliaments" which means Bill has been as "Atomic Dog." In fact, while Donald was building skyscrapers, Bill was moving birds through the chicken companies chasing real paper.

That's where the world renown term "Moving Birds" comes from. When Donald was drawing up his future as on "Apprentice" Bill was retired from dodging life sentences. Bill finally took over "The White House" with elegant "pimpery" he was smooth. Yet kept America united "One Nation Under a Groove."

Dumb Donald clown like Ronald
not Reagan, talking bout' McDonalds.
Try'n to skate again
Seal America fate again
More worst Making America Hate Again!

Trump is planning to do so by appealing to the mindset of the Neo-Nazi and hate organizations. Who have an agenda to fulfill which is to be dominate Industrious wise and be racially superior of all leaderships of the world. Trump and Vladimir Putin who comes from the Adolf Hitler school of thought are on this quest. Trump has shown and proved to us time after time that he's not fully emersed in the interest of American values for its citizens. This was displayed one of many times when Trump was asked.

"Do you think Russia hacked their way into our election?"

He responded from behind a podium at an international press conference. While Vladimir Putin was standing right next to him. He gripped the top of the box in a nervously lying politician style. He took a deep breath and said, "I asked Mr. Putin if it was him who hacked into our election. He said no it wasn't him. I don't think he has a reason to lie to me or to do something like that."

This was after all the U.S. intelligence agencies found that the hacking IP address had been traced to a Russian server.

Trump had already been in bed with Putin long before this. In a press conference shortly after Trump with Putin, Putin was asked by a female journalist on a stage in an auditorium filled to capacity with stone faced Russian men. "Are you going to get involved in the United States 2020 election process?"

Un-stunned, well poised without flinching the Russian dictator placed a hand to his cheek. The way you would when telling someone a secret, then said, "Yes, I am but don't tell anyone."

The audience roared in laughter at the same time for three to four seconds then stopped on a dime. Almost as if everyone felt that she asked a rhetorical question or riddle that everyone knew the answer to but her.

So, imagine Rudy and President Don Wann romancing some pretty Ukrainian women. They have an eight-block secured perimeter enforced by yours truly a small U.S. military team. They're tucked away at the DuTrump Inn a hotel 10 miles south of the Ukrainian / Russian war front.

Ukrainian President Volodymyr Zelensky has been given clearance to enter their area. He's battered and bruised with a once white now blood stained and heavily soiled bandana covers his entire head. With an AK-47 in his right hand and army fatigues that were made by Unicore the federal prisoners work detail in Beaumont, Texas. He's awed by the plushness of the décor that's a 180 from the lobby and rooms that he has slept in when tricking with young girls over the years.

He entered the state-of-the-art presidential suite. When he stepped around the foyer the room opened displaying Italian marble floors ensigned with gold T's. High quality Versace furniture, glass tables a rotating picture gram screen of major Trump hotels form around the world. That changes every three minutes showing the beauty of their night lights and skylines.

Volodymyr Zelensky achingly looked up at the high ceilings that suspended a dimly lit crystal and gold chandelier that's three feet in diameter and four feet in height.

Trump sat in the king's chair behind a fifthteen foot glass table that accompanied four rolling leather chairs on each side. Where a blond haired, white House aide, is transfixed on the laptop to Trump's left. Giuliani was in the hot tub across the room three Ukrainian women sitting on the tub's edges feeding him grapes and strawberries. Rudy hadn't had this much fun or attention since his bar mitzvah.

No one noticed Volodymyr Zelensky until Rudy bellowed, "Hey Volo come on in the water is great. The Ukrainian women sure know how to show good hospitality to your very special guest. Thank You!" Rudy laughed devilishly before the stuffing of more fruit shut him up.

Volodymyr stood looking at the kitchen area countertops. Which were just as beauteous as the floors but had gold trim, that was topped with gourmet foods on silver platters. A turkey that seen its better days, the ham had its bone cut and out and fruits and vegetables at the other end. One could tell it was a 5-star display that had been devoured by Team Trump. The Ukrainian President stared at Trump with pity me please eyes.

"Z Man how are you my good friend?" Trump asked. As he stood to his feet walking toward Zelensky.

"Not so good Mr. Trump. The Russians are coming! The Russians are coming invading us. We low on artillery, da tanks outdated, drones done get high enough. Once we get a view of the Russians location, they shoot the drone down. We need more javelins. I don't understand how you can be cool with Vladimir Putin?"

Trump stared at him coldly as if it were blaspheming to mention his murderous puppeteer.

"He has hacked into the American election process and… and he is having peepal kilt as we speak dis instant. Who are dees peepal?"

"Whoa, whoa, whoa!" Trump stated with open palms pushing at Volo. Trump towered the much shorter Ukrainian with a navy-blue Armani suit, white shirt, red tie from his own line. His signature dry neatly manicured toupee remained froze no matter how much he moved his head and hands.

"I asked Putin did he do it? He said he didn't do it. I believe him he has no reason to lie to me. Besides, I didn't need him to beat Hillary. I don't need any one to beat any woman." Said Trump matter of factly with puckered lips. "Besides nobody knows how to handle women better than me. I just grab'em by the pussy, and it's over with, I get'em. As for these people I got good people on both sides. Over there on the laptop fixing all of my factless frauds is Mrs. Kelly Ann Conway. "Kelly please stand and give Volo here a nice model strut for me please".

Kelly Ann did as directed almost before Trump could finish asking her. Looked in the direction of Volo and said. "Make America Hate Again! Make America Hate Again! Make America Hate Again!"

While sluggishly walking towards Volo at a snail's pace, showing her shapeuous tanned figure with a slow spin. Then displayed her pearly gleaming smile and went back to her seat.

"American made and her husband hates me. Then over there in the hot tub with the beautiful Ukrainian women is none other, my brother from a different Brother, my attorney, my good friend and ex-mayor of New York City, Rudeee Giuliani." Said Trump in a Michael Buffer ring announcer fashion.

Pudy Rudy as his childhood friends called him was compensating for the jacuzzies broken jets had his face buried in the water blowing bubbles, treading his hands by his ears like a dog. Yet managed to hear his accolades gave himself a wet round of applause. The Ukrainian playmates laughed uncontrollably at the childlike behavior from a man old enough to be their grandfathers' father. Volo on the other hand gave a sigh of disbelief, looked at Trump and cut the chase.

"What about the four hundred million we were approved to receive from the American Congress months ago. What's the hold up?"

"What do you know about sloppy Joe?"

"That's American food, "right"? With a look of incredulous on his face Volo asked. He limped two steps Trumps way then said, "What does food have to do with n-e-thing?"

In a painful tone he followed up. "My peepal are at war with Russia and they are killing us on all fronts. And this…" He moved his left arm around aimlessly while looking at Rudy and the girls. Stopped in midsentence. "Is that my niece in the tub?"

Rudy pushed one of the playmates head under the water. Volo brushed it off then focused back on Trump. Who had his arms folded across his chest waiting to rebuttal the Ukrainian's four hundred million dollar pitch. "I need the low down dirty information on Joe Biden and his son. He's going to be running against me in the 2020 election. I can't afford to lose with all the crooked shit I've done, I'm going to get arrested. It's been said that he was doing business over here through his son. I'm going to put a smear campaign on him like I did with Hillary Clinton.

" I thought you said you didn't…"

"Hey, it is what it is! A little dirt doesn't hurt."

"So, you say I get you dirt on Joe… "Sloppy Joe" as you call him. I get the four hundred million that has already been approved to us by Congress. Why you play games with Putin trying to overtake my Kuntry?"

"Let's just say it like you scratch my back I scratch yours type of deal. I'm not playing any type of games with you. In fact, I watched documentaries on some good people. Like Mussolini, Stalin, and my main man Hitler. So, if it's three things I know it's…"

Donald stretched his arms out to adjust his cuff links and then gave a finger for each.

"… Never mess with your mother-in-law, mother nature or a motherfucking Ukrainian."

Volo clearly blown away by Trumps "ba-foolery" wagged his head then in a flat dry tone said.

"I seen da movie you go dat from Mr. Trump."

Trump grimaced his face cut questioning eyes at Volo. "So, you have Netflix? Great film, right? Mark Wahlberg is a genius like me nobody knows genius more than me."

"Den you mention those murderous men like Hitler. Dey kilt more peepal den der are fish in da sea."

Trump interjected, "Wait a minute now if your talking about the Dead Sea everything is already dead."

"You get my point Mr. Trump! No one has the right to take a life but God. Dose men acted like dey were Gods."

On cue Pudy Rudy's head popped up from the tub with red framed black tinted U.S. Olympic swimmers' goggles. Drawing both men's attention. He raised his dripping hands, shook his palms to the sky. As Christians do in Baptist Churches then said.

"He may not be God! But for four hundred million dollars... Praise'em anyhow!"

"Yeah, praise me anyhow." said Trump carelessly shrugging his shoulders.

THE SCANDALOUS EVANGELIST

August 14, 1862, Abraham Lincoln said to our Black pastors: "You and we are different races. We have between us a broader difference than exists between almost any other two races. Your race suffers very greatly, many of them by living among us, while ours suffer from your presence."

I have a difficult time believing this guy would be responsible for freeing slaves. Let Trump tell it he's done, "Just as much if not more for Black people than Abraham Lincoln."

As a slave witnessing murder, rape, beatings and lynching of your loved ones. If someone told you Hitler was responsible for your freedom, you'd give him full credit. You are happy to be free, desperation is natures cheapest perfume, and it does not care who wears it. The Trump supporters don't measure his success by what he does for them, and some may be reluctant to honestly say to what great lengths they wouldn't go for him. They measure him by what he does or says to other people they don't like they consider their enemies. That's how they see him as successful even as a Christian. "Trumpmatized" supporters buck everything. Even requirements to wear face masks when required to do so. They are irrational in their views, even when it comes at their own expense.

Mr. Trump is purported to be a "billionaire" who hides his tax returns. He claims that he is a "genius," yet he hides his college grades. He is a big businessman, yet he bankrupted three casinos and lost more than $1 billion in 10 year. He boasts of being a "playboy" and beauty contest owner, yet he has paid multiple women for sex. He brags of is philanthropy but was ruled against in court for defrauding his own charity. He calls himself a "patriot" yet he avoided the draft five times during the Vietnam War era. Lastly he claims to be a "Christian," he can barely quote any scriptures and his only visit to a church this year was a for a photo opt outside the church just one block from the White House, where the bishop there said he was not welcome. I've heard Trump himself say, "I am the chosen one." I've also heard people that are "Trumpmatized" and been baptized in his Holy Shit say that "He's like as messiah or Jesus of the Christ."

I just look at them in total disbelief and say, "You know he very well maybe! Because he wants you to die for his sins."

Please America beware we have a very dangerous desperate president in office. His losing will have serious deadly consequences. We are already seeing civil unrest. Leave no complacency in your mind Trump will not take losing easily he never has but who does? There has been bloodshed of many Americans who hate and love Trump. In the end he and his rich friends will win, they don't care about you as long as they win. It's their plan to, "Making America Hate Again."

THE RALLY

So imagine a planned hush White Supremacy /"Trump Action Rally" being held in South Eastern Kentucky. Through a valley over a mountain sits Big Sandy United States Penitentiary, in Inez population 623. The prison like many barely rural towns is the economic crutch otherwise Inez would not exist.

The midday sun seemed ten feet above the mountainous earth, that yesterday's buckets of rainfall left spongey. A distinctive aroma of free Kentucky fried chicken guides you by the nose up the only road posting Trump decorates and paraphernalia to "The Rally in The Valley" hosted by yours truly, Mitch McConnell.

KKK Grand Wizard David Duke and Newt Gingrich sat on the main stage. Stretching the entire length of the platform a step and repeat wall. Displaying swastikas, "Make America Hate Again" provided by Home Depot, decals every 3 feet. This is to be McConnell's forever Trumper debut. Neo Nazi skin headed leaders flew in from as far as Germany and New Zealand bringing the total attendance to 75 people. Thirty-three of them were Secret Service. Although it was more pounds of roasted pigs, confederate flags, and gallon of gas to burn crosses than there were people the show must go on.

Rescue carried by two cadets from the presidential SUV across the muddy field, fearing his leather bottoms would be ruined Trump took the podium.

"Where's everyone at?" asked Trump covering the mic looking back a Duke and Newt. Both men aimed eyes at McConnell.

Through twisted lips Duke responded, "Operation hush. Said our base is tired of us not wearing mask during the Corona Bologna."

Left front viewer Paula Dean sat snug with a punk rocker blonde chick who is wearing a "Meth Labs Matter" t-shirt.

"I see you're still cooking Paula. Even after you lost all your endorsements. That was a sad, sad case for you Paula. You said one little word that starts with a N...," pinching is right index and thumb together. "One little word. They say it to each other all the time. I say N' words all the time, Neo-Nazi, Nationalist, it's nothing. People are so freaking technical these days. When everything is already perfect... Perfect, just like the phone call, it was perfect." Noting the frozen "Trumpmatized" temperature of his attendees Trump mashed the gas. "They love to test your patience or make you the patient they want to test you all the time. They need " He paused to add emphasis looking left to right. "That's another N' word. They need to stop testing. They want to test... tes, tes, tes. They say we don't wear our mask and we will spread the Corona Virus. We don't just wear our mask we wear our entire hoods. He said pounding on the podium

The sweet sixteen birthday party sized crowd erupted with whistles, white power, cowboy yells and Hail Trump arms stretched out in front of them. Trump then focused on Rosanne Bar who sat next to Paula Deans Miss Meth America date. Rosanne sporting a red "MAGA" hat, white tee Trump 2020 stenciled on with blue jeans, black mud caked knee highs. Because the two cadets refused to carry her fat ass as they did Trump, even after being offered two "Purple Hearts" a piece.

Trump eyed her coolly, "Hey Rosanne I'm still here. What is he a tax deductible?"   Referring to a man who was bowling ball black and bald, who sat on Rosanne's left. Clearly, nearly 90, with hearing aids in both ears, black shades and an orange tipped blind stick. He sat spaced transfixed.

"Oh, I get it… Hear no, see no and speak no evil. Right Rosanne?"

Wildly shaking her head chewing gum. "No that's not it dumb Donald."

"Well you may want to change his diaper cause there's a few flies around him. Oohhh! I get it… I get it! Blackballed, you've been blackballed. Is that the message behind your shenanigan's today?"

Rosanne burst a bubble, "Finally!"

"This is a very interesting row of characters here. And who is the cute little guy with his hood and robe on?" asked Trump.

"White power! Hail Trump! White Power!" Yelled the four-foot figure.

"That's my boy Mister Prezdent. Proud to be American's, we's call'em Lil'Hate". Said a hooded voice three rows back.

"Lil' Hate, there is nothing wrong with a Lil' Hate sometimes". Trump established.

"Yep!" Agreed Big Hate. "He and I are the one's sponsible to get'n people at the voting polls just as Governor McConnell ax us to dew...."

McConnell felt a bit of relief when Trump gave him a good job glance after today's disastrous turnout.

... "That's right Mister Trump me and Lil' Hate did one better. We's bought the polls to the people. They're over yonder that field!"

Big Hate directed everyone's attention to a pile of red and blue painted poles that had vote written on them along with clumps of other scrap metals and rods, that was eight feet high and fifteen feet round.

"That's a lot of poles." Trump quipped, revisiting McConnell who was within earshot.

"I'm never going to get re-elected if I depend on you Bitch McConnell. I see if your people can't fix it they'll nigger rig it."

"We wouldn't miss you for a mountainside of doublewides. Lil' Hate wanted to be front row at the show Mister Trump."

Trump put on a fictious smile, "I do put on a hell of a show don't I? Nobody puts on a better show than me. I have always been a talent over experience type of guy. Look at me..."

He threw his hands to the sky did a 1970's pimp spin on his right heel, stepped on a dime and stamped his left foot to the stage loudly, popped his head to the side in an Elvis Presley fashion then said, "We gotta win this race."

Gleefully rising to their feet, the ensemble sang. "Make America Hate Again… Make America Hate Again…"

Chippiously elated Duke, McConnell, Pence and associates gave each other high fives with fist balled slot machine pulls upstage of Trump. Who was feeling himself and hadn't uttered one supremacist or political agenda?

Puzzled faced Trump continued down the row. "Hey, I noticed that everyone is enjoying my show but you. Are you not entertained?" Doing an open armed ninety degree turn left to right. He stared at the bulkous design that sat crossed armed behind a brown sheet with black leather gloves and Long John sleeves.

"I'm here cuz I's heard it was a "Junk Auction Rally." You know one man's trash another man's treasure."

"Listen to me…" Pinching his fingers together Trump enunciated the words. "Trump Action Rally, don't you see all the action going on around me? There are people fighting to get in here. You got the…" Using finger quotes he continued on. "Equal Justice protestors, anti-protestors then you got the Corona testers. Tes, tes, tes, tes everybody wants to test. Lorena Bobbitt wanted to run test here for Covid-19, as part of her life term community service sanctions. By the way sanctions are good. She cut off her husband's testis, I told Lorena no I don't need you to take any test on me I'm fine."

Once Trump patted his palms towards the floor nearly silencing the "Trumpies" he turned to Mr. Brownsheets. Who was displaying an unimpressed body language of the key speaker's antics and punchlines?

"Gentlemen I believe we've found our Whistle-blower! Take your hood off."

"Nah, Nah, No!" Mr. Brownsheets stood to is feet started running wildly, jumping over empty seats.

Newt "Gangrich" standing in amazement said, "He gotta be black. Look at him run like a monkey. Nowhere to run to baby, nowhere to hide. That's Howard Cassell and Sly and the family. See! I know my history should 'a made me Vice Trump."

Two confederate Flag painted rocks on a rope were hurled across the air wrapping around the neck of Mr. Brownsheets, giving him a Cabbage Patch kid appearance. Brownsheets flattered as he flew into the Port-A-John causing the cap to spill next to is unconscious body. The thrower Mike Pence got face to face with Newt bounced with each syllable.

"Enny, Meany, Miny, Moe… Catch a nigger by the throat! That's why I am his vice."

"Good throw Mike." He and Trump bumped fist. Not taking his eyes off the three exposed bodies huddled by the ports toilet he asked. "Is that CNN?"

"No those aren't reporters sir." Pence confirmed.

"Yes, it is." Trump said convincingly. "That's Chuck Schumer, Nancy Boa Constrictor Pelosi and Greg No Neck Nadler. My God! They're always trying to stir some shit up. I guess they are in the right place now aren't they Mike? Both men laughing Trump yelled.

"I can save my fifty-thousand dollar bounty you brough him right to me didn't you Nancy?"

"No. He's not with us, we're here getting more evidence to impeach your ass. You're finished after this Klan rally Trump."

Nadler announced as the trio headed to the stage.

"So ya'll decided to join the Klan?" Paula Dean asked happily.

"No, we had to dress this way to get in." Chuck Schumer reasoned.

Several Klansmen hurriedly gathered Mr. Brownsheets lifeless frame. Dropped with the care of a sack of potatoes Brownsheets gained consciousness from his head hitting a chairs leg he sat up.

"This is pure political theater. Incredible, nowhere in America can you get this much excitement on one hill." McConnell claimed.

"Capital Hill!"

"So we can agree on something huh fancy Nancy? Unmask that man." McConnell commanded.

Trump and company hawkeyed on an oval face military muscle who rushed to do thee honor. A frail puny man wearing a Bass Pro Shop hat yelled through rotten jagged edged teeth.

"OJ what? You're here for the free chicken ain't ya boy? The fuck your black ass doing here?"

Dizzily responding, "I'm not black... I'm OJ. I came..."

Before he could complete another thought Oval face punched OJ back to sleep, then backhand bitch slapped him awake. Other's followed Lil' Hate kicks, stomps and elbows to the head. Beating OJ to a pulp, juice was leaking everywhere.

Feeling somewhat sorry for OJ, Chuck Schumer screamed, "Ok, that's enough, that's a mutha' freakin' nough'! You guys are going to kill'em."

There was a moment of silence until Lil' Hate gave one last kick and ran back to is seat. OJ helplessly looked around confused bleeding profusely from the cut over his right eye.

"Chuck, Nancy, Nadler what... What are you guys doing here? I thought you were democrats' good ones not Klansmen... well, and Woman" OJ said looking at Pelosi.

She forced through a wedge of hate mongers squat beside OJ, grabbed a fist full of her robes bottom and blotted his wound.

"You're going to need stitches for this... OJ what are you doing here?"

OJ didn't sound like the intelligent SC graduate. Or the ex-sports commentator. He sounded like... like... a slave.

"Nancy, I's wuz get'n me's a coffee at Denny's and I's overheard him's talking behind me's. They did'n know I's wuz dare..." All eyes on OJ intently as he appealed for understanding. He continued with a quivering tone. "One's dem' men said sumptin' bout' a, "Hush Junk Auction Rally" here in Inez. I's worked my's ass off for dems' trophies. I's did time for dem'... I's just want my's stuff."

Feeling no compassion for OJ shaking his head Trump went in, "Unbelievable. You're a pathetic con artist OJ. This is a, 'Trump Action Rally'! You haven't been paying attention to what's going on have you OJ? Your people," Trump paused... "Not just blacks but people all over the world have been knocking down monuments. You have the audacity to come here with that fake coon shit. When people worldwide have been toppling over my heritage, the statues of my forefathers. Do you think anybody gives a damn about your trophies?"

Loudly clearing is throat Lil' Hates daddy raised a finger. "Aye, uhh Mister Trump... I looked at all the pictures in all your books. I didn't see you had four fathers." He displayed four fingers. "Your mama must've been a..."

"Shut your stupid ass mouth!" Interjected unhooded red robed Roger Stone, giving his fearless leader a ritual high fire chased by walking their fingertips upward.

"Where to boss?"

"All the way up." Trump countered without breaking interest from CNN.

"Gotcha!" Assuredly Stone nodded.

Still on the impeachment fishing expedition Schumer opened the dialog. "Trump you have been involved in scandalous messes since you stepped foot in the White House. We can start as far back as 'The Stormy Daniels Scandal! How did things work out with Stormy?"

"Stormy! More like a Tsnami I paid over a hundred grand for that pussy. And she didn't keep her mouth shut.

Guess in her line of work you don't get paid if you keep it shut..."

Trump switched positions from standing on the stages edge to leaning his left arm on the podium for comfort.

"You know how it goes Chuck, players fuck up. Players do fuck up. I'm a big golfer, I love playing golf nobody plays more golf than me. I play at all of my resorts, Links at Ferry Point. The Mar-a-Largo Club in Florida. Trump World Golf Club in Dubai which is one of my favorite places to play."

"What does golfing have to do with women and prostitutes like Stormy Daniels?" Curiously asked Nadler.

Throwing his face towards the clouds nearly falling backwards dancing, spaghetti waving his arms behind himself Trump hollered, "I love them hoes."

Again, loads of laughs came from all of Trumps men. After fully catching his breath he eyed each addressee as he spoke.

"Chuck, Nancy and No Neck Nadler. We as a nation have been fucking over people and other countries since the beginning of time. The blacks had it we tricked them into slavery. That was over four hundred years ago, they still haven't recovered. I don't think that they own a deed to a diamond mine in their own homeland or a warehouse here in America. They built America and are owed reparations from over 12 generations. The same goes for the Mexicans hard working talented people. We don't want to make the mistake of letting them know their true value. They master ingenuity my wall couldn't keep them out. The wall fiasco was a big hoax they went under it in tunnels. However, it was very financially lucrative for me and my team."

A rhythmical roar of helicopters from somewhere over the blue grass mountains could be heard approaching. Chuck Schumer surveyed Trump who was straightening his clothes, with disgust in his eyes for the president. Schumer unleashed.

"So, Trump you made millions off of the wall didn't you?"

Trump looked at Schumer as if that were a trick question. Tilted his head and listed to the man's tirade.

"You pitched the idea to your racist base who was already on division time. Got your people probably some contractors you've dealt with in the past on a few of your hotels…" Schumer glanced at Nadler who had lost the blood flow in his face due to his anger, then at Pelosi who had tears in her eyes, then grossly back to Trump. "They over charge the public, give you a kick back funneled through one of your shell corps and you win again."

"Bingo Chucky! You win totally nothing! We could continue to win if you democrats would join forces with me. We would implement a, "Trump World Order" where big business owners would take care of their people and we give the brown and trailer trash whites the crumbs, which they're used to anyway".

Several of the base members looked offended by his words. Uncaring he rambled on.

"I'm a demagogue, I played on their likes and appealed to my bases emotions in order to gain political power. In this case I told them the Mexicans were taking all their jobs. Although they do the jobs nobody wants to do anyway. Warehouse and hard labor which will keep the uneducated whites at odds with the Mexicans. As for the blacks we keep them in check with over prosecution, lengthy prison sentences and police brutality. This way we kill two birds with one stone. We slow down their reproductive rates and keep the fear of God in them in their own neighborhoods. But as you have been seeing. The blacks are getting tired of getting their asses whipped and murdered. It's a big cluster fuck that was here long before me. I just happen to be the recipient of past practices with gold opportunities."

"So just turn everyone against each other while you and your people ride off into the sunset. Is that your plan Donald? What about change for Americans' or humanity as a whole?" Pelosi pleaded.

"How about we get the money, and you can keep your change. The Mexicans are invading America, and the Chinese are mad that I taxed their GDP's. So, what did they do in retaliation?" He looked around at his mystery faced listeners for answers. After a full thirty seconds of blank stares, shoulder shrugs and tilted hoods he spat.

"They released the Corona Virus, the Kung Flu. Bats my ass!" Trump rolled his head in rage. "Those chinks are smart. Pretty soon America will be called "Brown Town". We'll have Kool-Aid, burritos, and egg rolls on every dinner table across the country. And I'm not letting that go down. I'll blow it up before I let any of them have it. It's a good thing they just wanna protest and march. Instead of getting out and vote or I'd be in trouble."

CNN observed the nods, consternation, the seriousness of the "Trumpmatized" audience. Then a strange mystical aura overtook all the Trump sublines. Even with three Siekierski Helicopters hovering above their heads they were deer in headlights, unmoving.

"Get to the chopper. Get to the chopper now!" The pilot declared.

Trump had a left hand holding his hair down, pointing upward with his right looking at CNN who at once yelled, "Arnold?"

Roger Stone caught the choppers harness that reminds you of a legless baby onesie with a rope attached to its chest. He slid his hand over Trumps allowing the president to remove his hand quickly. The two cadets put Trump safely in the harness with a helmet on.

"He's such a baby he's only nine hundred and fifthteen months old." Pelosi humored.

"What about our country losing battles to the virus? Your base that's being De-Trumpmatized, and tired of hating?" Nadler blared.

"Look I tell my people we can't listen to Dr. Anthony Fauci. His science and methods stink Chuck Woolery from, "The Love Connection," I agree with him. Or take some hydroxychloroquine or bleach... drink some bleach."

"You're a psychopath Trump. What's that your Jim Jones theory?" Chuck questioned with unbelievability. Showing his palms yelling at the top of his lungs

"Take it... Just take it, what do you have to lose? You're gonna die anyway..." He moved on with a casualness. "... As for my people who turned away from being forever "Trumpsters" or "Trumpmatized."

Wagging a finger at those who stood tranced.

"Even my own niece said the way it looks I'm not well and diagnosed me certified crazy. I'm not into looks. I'm into pocketbooks. If I can't use'em, I lose'em, fuck'em."

Reeled in fast as yo-yo string. The aircrafts mouth swallowed shut then headed eastward.